Five Senses
Phonics

BOOK
1

Hunter Calder

A
FIVE SENSES
PUBLICATION

Five Senses Education Pty Ltd
2/195 Prospect Highway
Seven Hills NSW 2147 Australia
Phone   02 838 9265
Email   sevenhills@fivesenseseducation.com.au
Web   www.fivesenseseducation.com.au

Calder, Hunter
Five Senses Phonics Book 1
978-1-76032-422-3

2022 04 04

Contents

v   Introduction

vi   Instructions for Book 1

1–5   Sound Charts: Vowel and Consonant Sounds

6   Basic Sight Vocabulary

7–22   Unit 1: Rhyming Words

23–30   Unit 2: Initial Consonants

31–38   Unit 3: Terminal Consonants

39–46   Unit 4: Medial Vowels

47–54   Unit 5: Initial Consonants

55–62   Unit 6: Terminal Consonants

63–70   Unit 7: Medial Vowels

71–75   Unit 8: Vowel Revision

76–91   Achievement Tests

About the Author

Multiple award-winning author Hunter Calder has extensive experience as a reading teacher, consultant, teacher trainer and lecturer, both in Australia and overseas. He obtained a Master of Arts from the University of Sydney and a Master of Education from the University of New South Wales. His many publications include the acclaimed *Reading Freedom 2000* series and the *Excel Basic English* books. He also contributed to the *Literacy Planet* online program.

The *Five Senses Phonics* series of early literacy skills is his most recent series of phonics books and is the outcome of collaboration with the experienced people at Five Senses Education.

Introduction

Welcome to *Five Senses Phonics*, a carefully structured series of activity books for pre-readers and beginning readers at the important stage of their literacy acquisition. The Five Senses activity books are intended for use in a preschool setting, in the beginning school years, and for older students who are having difficulty learning to read.

Book 1 allows students to develop the essential precondition of reading — phonemic awareness. Phonemic awareness refers to a student's ability to hear and work with sounds in spoken words. Students with good phonemic awareness skills know that words contain sequences of individual sounds. They know, for instance, the sounds 'b' - 'a' - 't' blend together to form the word 'bat'. Contemporary research tells us that students with good phonemic awareness skills go on to become competent readers. On the other hand, preschool age children and students in the early years at school who do not understand the relationship between spoken and written words are likely to develop literacy problems. Students who experience difficulty learning the skills of phonemic awareness may need the services of a specialised teacher trained in the development of auditory perception techniques.

The exercises are structured to allow the student to progressively attain competence in the skills of phonemic awareness. On completing Book 1, students are able to apply these skills to discriminate individual sounds in words. Students then progress to Book 2 to consolidate their skills and develop alphabet knowledge.

Student progress should regularly be monitored and evaluated after completing each level, using the Achievement Tests section which is specifically designed for teachers to assess effectiveness and so students can see the positive results of their learning experiences.

Instructions for Book 1

Pages 1–5   **Vowel and consonant sounds** — teach these sounds carefully and until students can reproduce them automatically.

Page 6   **Phonics First sight vocabulary** — these lists contain the basic sight words students need to work successfully with Phonics First. Teach the words list by list until they are mastered. Teach or revise the words as they are presented at the bottom of each page.

Pages 7–14   **Rhyming words** — students say the words for the pictures and circle 'yes' if the words rhyme and 'no' if they don't.

Pages 15–22   **Rhyming words** — students say the words for the pictures and circle the words that rhyme.

Pages 23–30   **Initial consonants** — students circle the picture that begins with the sound for the letter in the column beside it.

Pages 31–38   **Terminal consonants** — students circle the picture that ends with the sound for the letter in the column beside it. Explain that even though a word like 'cave' ends with the letter 'e' the last sound they hear is 'v', so for 'cave' the letter to be circled is 'v'.

Pages 39–46   **Vowel sounds** — students are to circle the picture that contains the sound of the vowel in the column beside it.

Pages 47–54   **Initial consonants** — students look at the picture and circle the letter of the beginning sound they hear.

Pages 55–62   **Terminal consonants** — students look at the picture and circle the letter of the ending sound they hear.

Pages 63–70   **Vowel sounds** — students look at the picture and circle the letter of the vowel sound they hear.

Pages 71–75   **Vowel revision** — students draw a line from the vowel sound to the pictures with the same vowel sound.

Pages 76–90   **Achievement Tests** — students complete the test to demonstrate mastery.

Sound Charts

Single Letter-Sound Correspondences: Vowels

Say the sounds for these letters.

a as in

e as in

i as in

o as in

U as in

(1)

Sound Charts

Say the sounds for these letters.

b   as   in

c   as   in

d   as   in

f   as   in

g   as   in

2

Sound Charts

Single Letter-Sound Correspondences: Consonants

Say the sounds for these letters.

h   as   in

j   as   in

k   as   in

l   as   in

m   as   in

③

Sound Charts

Say the sounds for these letters.

n   as   in

p   as   in

r   as   in

s   as   in

t   as   in

4

Sound Charts

Single Letter-Sound Correspondences: Consonants

Say the sounds for these letters.

V   as   in

W   as   in

X   as   in

y   as   in

z   as   in

Basic Sight Vocabulary

Learn these lists of sight words

a	in	and	saw	into	this
am	is	are	she	play	what
as	it	for	the	said	when
by	Mr	her	too	then	will
he	no	him	was	they	with
if	of	Mrs	why		
	on	not	yes		
		out	you		

Unit 1:1

Circle **yes** if the words rhyme and **no** if they don't.

    yes   no

    yes   no

    yes   no

    yes   no

    yes   no

a   am   as   by   (7)

Unit 1:2

Circle **yes** if the words rhyme and **no** if they don't.

		yes	no
		yes	no
		yes	no
		yes	no
		yes	no

(8)   a   am   as   by

Unit 1:3

Circle **yes** if the words rhyme and **no** if they don't.

    yes   no

    yes   no

    yes   no

    yes   no

    yes   no

a   am   as   by   9

Circle **yes** if the words rhyme and **no** if they don't.

  yes   no

  yes   no

  yes   no

  yes   no

  yes   no

 a   am   as   by

Unit 1:5

Circle **yes** if the words rhyme and **no** if they don't.

  yes no

  yes no

  yes no

  yes no

  yes no

a   am   as   by   (11)

Unit 1:6

Circle **yes** if the words rhyme and **no** if they don't.

	yes	no
	yes	no
	yes	no
	yes	no
	yes	no

(12)   a   am   as   by

Unit 1:7

Circle **yes** if the words rhyme and **no** if they don't.

  yes　　no

  yes　　no

  yes　　no

  yes　　no

  yes　　no

a　　　　am　　　　as　　　　by　　(13)

Circle **yes** if the words rhyme and **no** if they don't.

    yes   no

    yes   no

    yes   no

    yes   no

    yes   no

(14)   a   am   as   by

Unit 1:9

Circle the two words that rhyme.

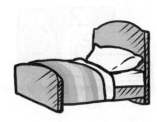  

he   if   in   is   it   (15)

Circle the two words that rhyme.

(16) he if in is it

Circle the two words that rhyme.

he   if   in   is   it   17

Circle the two words that rhyme.

(18) he   if   in   is   it

Circle the two words that rhyme.

he   if   in   is   it   (19)

Circle the two words that rhyme.

20 he   if   in   is   it

Unit 1:15

Circle the two words that rhyme.

he   if   in   is   it   (21)

Circle the two words that rhyme.

(22)   he   if   in   is   it

Circle the the picture that **begins** with this sound.

t

v

y

w

b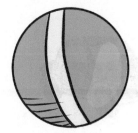

Mr   no   of   on   and   (23)

Circle the picture that **begins** with this sound.

z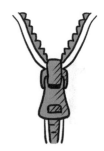

b

c

d

f

(24) Mr   no   of   on   and

Circle the picture that **begins** with this sound.

g         

j         

h         

l         

k         

Mr   no   of   on   and   (25)

Circle the picture that **begins** with this sound.

n

m

s

p

r

(26) Mr   no   of   on   and

Unit 2:5

Circle the picture that **begins** with this sound.

z         

b      

c         

d         

f         

Mr   no   of   on   and   (27)

Circle the picture that **begins** with this sound.

t

v

r

w

d

Mr   no   of   on   and

Unit 2:7

Circle the picture that **begins** with this sound.

g

j

h

l

k

Mr   no   of   on   and   29

Circle the picture that **begins** with this sound.

n

m

s

p

r

(30) Mr   no   of   on   and

Unit 3:1

Circle the picture that **ends** with this sound.

b         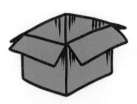

d         

f         

g         

k         

are   for   her   him   Mrs   (31)

Circle the picture that **ends** with this sound.

| l |  |  |  |

| p |  |  |  |

| m |  |  |  |

| r |  |  |  |

| n |  |  |  |

(32)   are   for   her   him   Mrs

Unit 3:3

Circle the picture that **ends** with this sound.

s

v

t

x

b

are   for   her   him   Mrs   (33)

Circle the picture that **ends** with this sound.

f       

d       

g       

l       

k       

(34)   are   for   her   him   Mrs

Unit 3:5

Circle the picture that **ends** with this sound.

s         

r         

p         

n         

m         

are   for   her   him   Mrs   35

Circle the picture that **ends** with this sound.

X

V

t

d

b

(36) are   for   her   him   Mrs

Circle the picture that **ends** with this sound.

f         

g         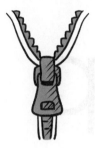

k         

m         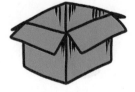

l         

are   for   her   him   Mrs   37

Circle the picture that **ends** with this sound.

n			
p			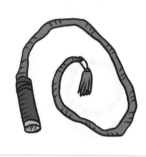
r			
s			
t			

(38)   are   for   her   him   Mrs

Circle the picture that has this **vowel** sound.

a   

e   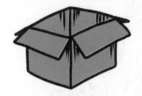

i   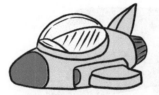

o   

u   

not   out   saw   she   the   39

Circle the picture that has this **vowel** sound.

not   out   saw   she   the

Circle the picture that has this **vowel** sound.

a

e

i

o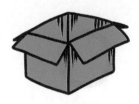

u

not　　out　　saw　　she　　the　　(41)

Circle the picture that has this **vowel** sound.

a			
e			
i			
o			
u			

(42)   not   out   saw   she   the

Circle the picture that has this **vowel** sound.

a

e

i

o

u

not   out   saw   she   the   43

Unit 4:6

Circle the picture that has this **vowel** sound.

a

e

i

o

u

not   out   saw   she   the

Unit 4:7

Circle the picture that has this **vowel** sound.

a

e

i

o

u

not   out   saw   she   the   (45)

Circle the picture that has this **vowel** sound.

a

e

i

o

u

(46) not   out   saw   she   the

Unit 5:1

What sound does this picture **begin** with? Circle the letter.

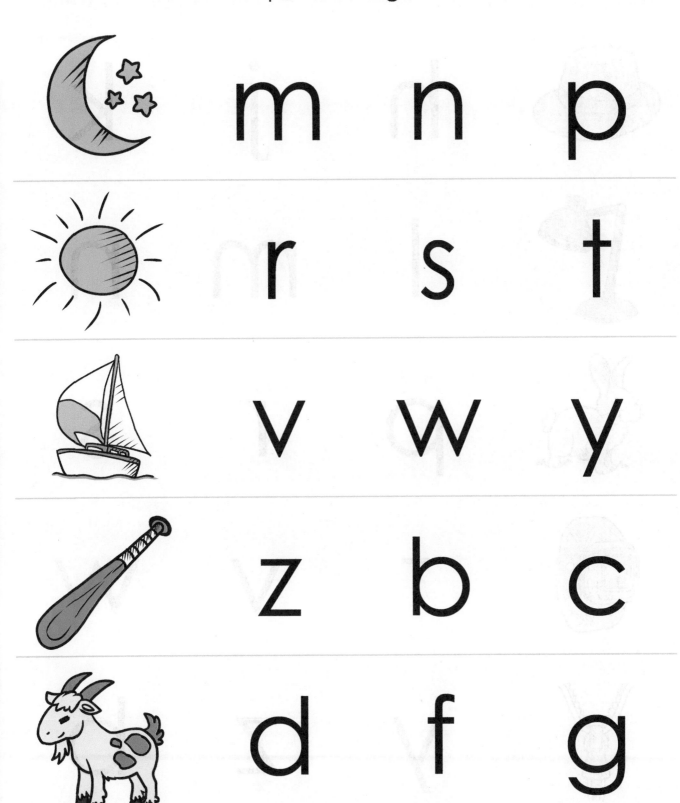

m	n	p
r	s	t
v	w	y
z	b	c
d	f	g

too   was   why   yes   you   47

What sound does this picture **begin** with? Circle the letter.

h   j   k

l   m   n

p   r   s

t   v   w

y   z   b

(48)   too   was   why   yes   you

What sound does this picture **begin** with? Circle the letter.

   c   d   f

   g   h   j

   l   m   k

   r   p   n

   v   s   t

too   was   why   yes   you   49

What sound does this picture **begin** with? Circle the letter.

   z   y   t

   f   d   g

   w   c   p

   n   m   l

   s   r   h

(50)   too   was   why   yes   you

Unit 5:5

What sound does this picture **begin** with? Circle the letter.

 m   n   p

 r   s   t

 v   w   y

 z   b   c

 d   f   g

What sound does this picture **begin** with? Circle the letter.

h	j	k
l	m	n
p	r	s
t	v	w
y	z	b

(52) too   was   why   yes   you

What sound does this picture **begin** with? Circle the letter.

c   d   f

g   h   j

l   m   k

r   p   n

v   t   s

too   was   why   yes   you   (53)

What sound does this picture **begin** with? Circle the letter.

z   r   w

f   d   g

k   j   h

n   l   m

r   d   p

54   too   was   why   yes   you

Unit 6:1

What sound does this picture **end** with? Circle the letter.

   b   d   f

   g   k   l

   m   n   p

   r   s   t

v   x   b

into   play   said   then   they   (55)

What sound does this picture **end** with? Circle the letter.

 d f g

 k l m

 n p r

 s t v

 x b d

(56) into   play   said   then   they

Unit 6:3

What sound does this picture **end** with? Circle the letter.

 g l k

 p s m

 t n r

 x g v

 d b f

into   play   said   then   they   57

Unit 6:4

What sound does this picture **end** with? Circle the letter.

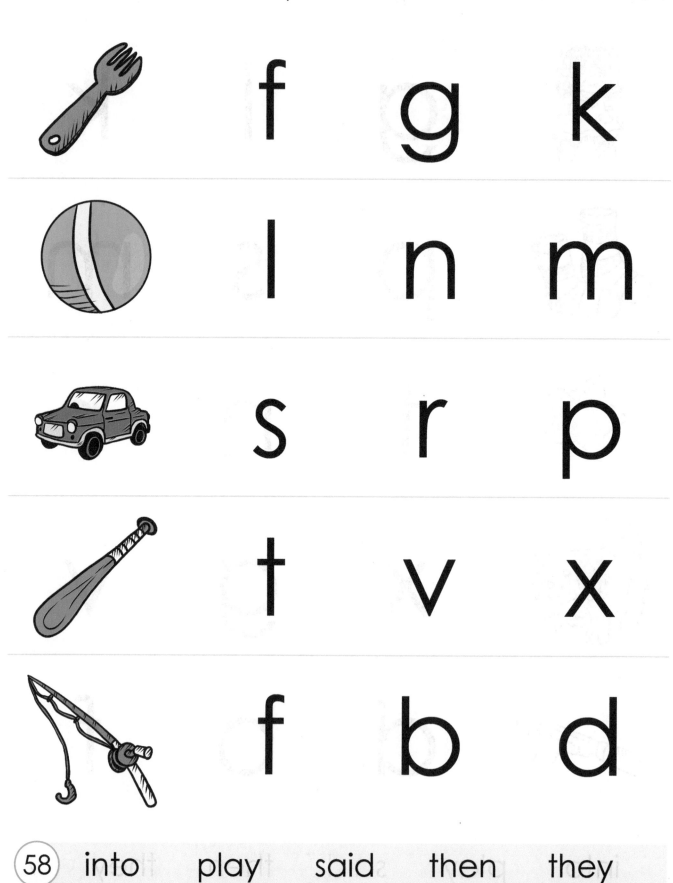

	f	g	k
	l	n	m
	s	r	p
	t	v	x
	f	b	d

into   play   said   then   they

What sound does this picture **end** with? Circle the letter.

　t　d　f

　g　k　l

　m　n　p

　r　s　t

　v　x　b

into　play　said　then　they　(59)

What sound does this picture **end** with? Circle the letter.

 d   m   g

 k   l   b

 n   p   r

 s   t   v

 x   m   d

60   into   play   said   then   they

Unit 6:7

What sound does this picture **end** with? Circle the letter.

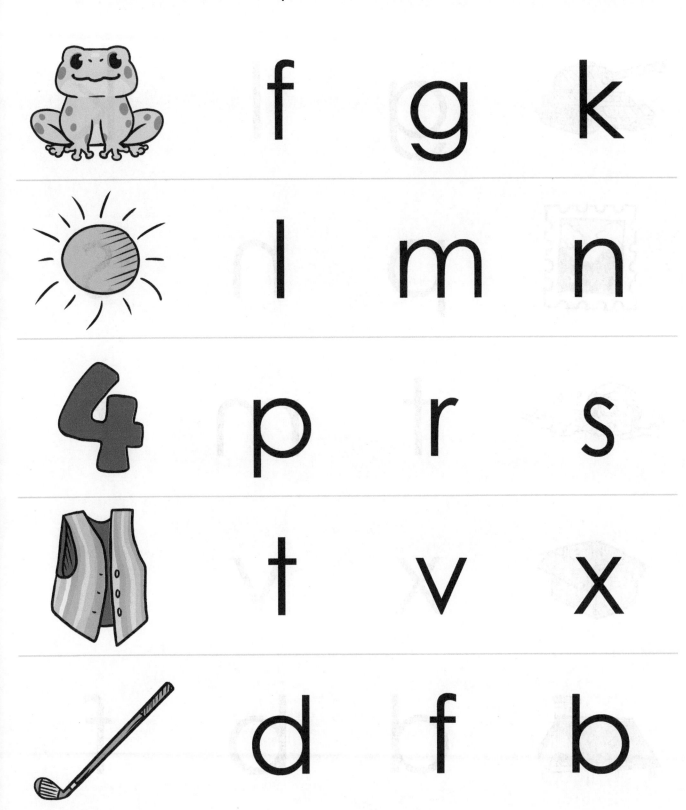

	f	g	k
	l	m	n
	p	r	s
	t	v	x
	d	f	b

into   play   said   then   they   61

Unit 6:8

What sound does this picture **end** with? Circle the letter.

 g   l   k

 p   n   s

 t   m   r

 x   v   l

 d   b   f

(62)   into   play   said   then   they

Circle the letter for the **vowel** sound.

Circle the letter for the **vowel** sound.

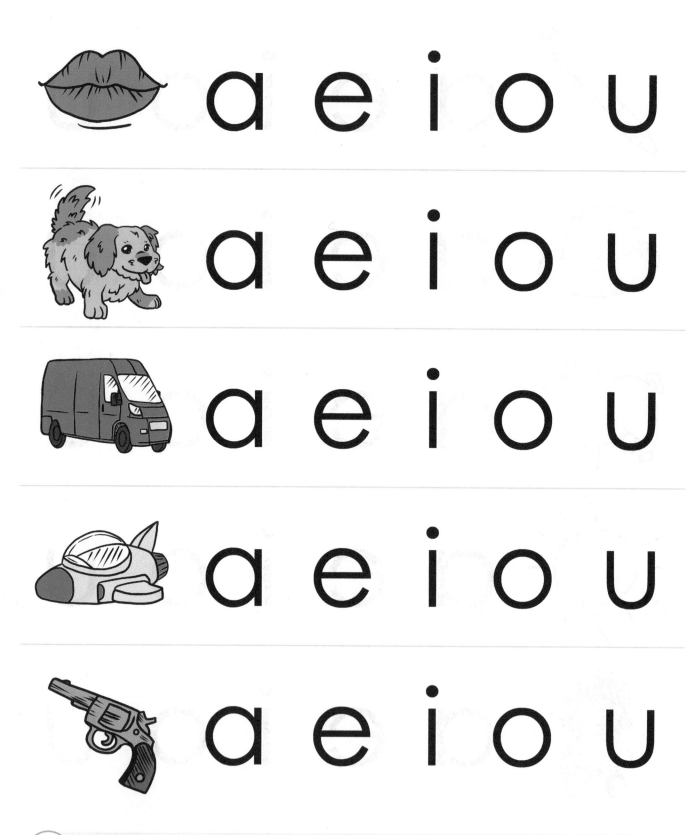

a e i o u

a e i o u

a e i o u

a e i o u

a e i o u

this   what   when   will   with

Circle the letter for the **vowel** sound.

 a e i o u

 a e i o u

 a e i o u

 a e i o u

 a e i o u

this   what   when   will   with   (65)

Circle the letter for the **vowel** sound.

a e i o u

a e i o u

a e i o u

a e i o u

a e i o u

this   what   when   will   with

Circle the letter for the **vowel** sound.

a e i o u

a e i o u

a e i o u

a e i o u

a e i o u

this   what   when   will   with   (67)

Circle the letter for the **vowel** sound.

a e i o u

a e i o u

a e i o u

a e i o u

a e i o u

this   what   when   will   with

Circle the letter for the **vowel** sound.

 a e i o u

 a e i o u

 a e i o u

 a e i o u

 a e i o u

this   what   when   will   with   (69)

Circle the letter for the **vowel** sound.

a e i o u

a e i o u

a e i o u

a e i o u

a e i o u

(70) this   what   when   will   with

Unit 8:1

Vowel Revision 1: Short 'a' Sound

Draw a line to the pictures that have an 'a' sound

Unit 8:2

Draw a line to the pictures that have an 'e' sound

Five Senses Phonics Book 1

Unit 8:3

Vowel Revision 3: Short 'i' Sound

Draw a line to the pictures that have an 'i' sound

Draw a line to the pictures that have an 'o' sound

Unit 8:5

Vowel Revision 5: Short 'u' Sound

Draw a line to the pictures that have an 'u' sound

Achievement Tests

The Five Senses Phonics Achievement Tests complement each book in the Five Senses Phonics series. They are specifically designed to enable teachers to ensure that what has been taught remains current in the student's repertoire of skills. They can then identify areas that need reteaching or reinforcement.

The format of each Five Senses Phonics Achievement Test is identical to the equivalent book so students encounter activities with which they are familiar. Each test evaluates skills and sight words students have been taught. The careful design of the tests, ensures that the monitoring of progress is a positive and non-threatening exercise.

For ease of administration, the tests are photocopiable. The class record sheets and student record sheets allow the teacher to scan student performance on an individual or whole class basis. Taken as a group, the tests give a running record of each student's skill acquisition of the phonic hierarchy. Teachers who teach reading systematically and record student progress methodically will find the Five Senses Phonics First Achievement Tests an indispensable part of their teaching routine.

How to use these tests

The Five Senses Phonics Achievement Tests are intended to be an encouraging record of progress, not an intimidating assessment. The tests can be administered to individual students or the entire class. Allow approximately 30 minutes to complete each test.

Each group of tests contains one or two sight vocabulary tests. If administering the test to the class as a whole, have individual students read groups of sight words, then ask the class to read all sight words together. Keep watch for children who are having trouble, and test them later individually.

Maintain a positive attitude while administering the tests, and reward success with stickers, stamps and merit certificates. To attain mastery students should obtain at least 80 marks out of a possible 100. Any areas in the Test that indicate weakness should be retaught and then reinforced.

Test Record Sheet

Student .... Date...

Page	Test		
78	1	Knowledge of Vowel Sounds	/ 5
79	2–5	Knowledge of Consonant Sounds	/20
83	6-7	Rhyming Words	/10
85	8	Initial Consonants	/ 5
86	9	Terminal Consonants	/ 5
87	10	Medial Vowels	/ 5
88	11	Initial Consonants	/ 5
89	12	Terminal Consonants	/ 5
90	13	Medial Vowels	/ 5
91	14	Knowledge of Basic Sight Vocabulary	/35

Total /100

Test 1:1

Draw a line to the picture with the vowel sound.

a

e

i

o

u

Score ☐ / 5

Test 1:2

Knowledge of Consonant Sounds

Draw a line to the picture with the consonant sound.

b

c

d

f

g

Score ⬚ / 5

Test 1:3

Knowledge of Consonant Sounds

Draw a line to the picture with the consonant sound.

h

j

k

l

m

80

Score | / 5

Test 1:4

Knowledge of Consonant Sounds

Draw a line to the picture with the consonant sound.

n

p

r

s

t

Score / 5

(81)

Test 1:5

Draw a line to the picture with the consonant sound.

v

w

x

y

z

Score / 5

Test 1:6

Circle **yes** if the words rhyme and **no** if they don't.

  yes   no

  yes   no

  yes   no

  yes   no

  yes   no

Score | / 5

Test 1:7

Circle the two words that rhyme.

(84)

Score ☐ / 5

Test 1:8

Initial Consonants

Circle the picture that **begins** with this sound.

d

j

p

z

b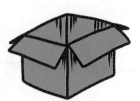

Score / 5

Test 1:9

Circle the picture that **ends** with this sound.

l			
n			
x			
m			
v			

Score / 5

Test 1:10

Circle the picture that has this **vowel** sound.

a

e

i

o

U

Score / 5

Test 1:11

What sound does this picture **begin** with? Circle the letter.

   l   m   k

   f   d   g

   t   r   s

   j   v   m

   w   y   p

(88)   **Score** ☐ / 5

Test 1:12

What sound does this picture **end** with? Circle the letter.

   x   g   v

   k   p   b

   r   d   n

   v   z   f

   m   l   p

Score ⬚ / 5

89

Test 1:13

Circle the letter for the **vowel** sound.

 a e i o u

 a e i o u

 a e i o u

 a e i o u

 a e i o u

Score ☐ / 5

Read these sight words

am	it	and	yes	into
he	of	not	why	then
by	no	him	too	what
if	in	out	the	this
as	for	you	said	will
is	her	saw	play	with
on	are	she	they	when

Score | / 35